KNOWING
WHO WE ARE:
LEADER GUIDE

KNOWING WHO WE ARE
The Wesleyan Way of Grace

Knowing Who We Are
978-1-7910-3203-6
978-1-7910-3202-9 eBook

Knowing Who We Are: Leader Guide
978-1-7910-3205-0
978-1-7910-3204-3 eBook

Knowing Who We Are: DVD
978-1-7910-3206-7

Who We Are And What We Believe:
50 Questions about The UMC
(a companion reader to the study)
978-1-7910-3208-1
978-1-7910-3207-4 eBook

Also by Laceye C. Warner

All the Good:
A Wesleyan Way of Christmas

The Method of Our Mission:
United Methodist Polity & Organization

Laceye C. Warner

KNOWING WHO WE ARE

The Wesleyan Way of Grace

WHAT WE BELIEVE, WHAT WE DO, AND WHY

Abingdon Press | Nashville

Knowing Who We Are:
The Wesleyan Way of Grace
Leader Guide

Copyright © 2024 Abingdon Press
All rights reserved.

978-1-7910-3205-0

MANUFACTURED IN THE UNITED STATES OF AMERICA

CONTENTS

CONTENTS

TO THE LEADER

Welcome! Thank you for accepting the invitation to serve as the facilitator for this study of *Knowing Who We Are: The Wesleyan Way of Grace* by Laceye C. Warner. In her introduction to the book the author states that "the purpose of this book is to offer those involved in church life a deeper understanding of the distinctives of Methodism to strengthen our sense of identity, better express our beliefs, and deepen our connections within The United Methodist Church." She writes that God's grace and sanctification are key beliefs in Wesleyan/Methodist theology.

This six-session study includes the following components:

- the book *Knowing Who We Are: The Wesleyan Way of Grace* by Laceye C. Warner;
- this Leader Guide; and
- video segments for each of the six chapters in the book, available via DVD or through the streaming service Amplify Media.

It will be helpful if participants obtain a copy of the book in advance and read chapter 1 before the first session. Each participant will need a Bible. It is recommended that participants also have a notebook or journal for taking notes, recording insights, and noting questions during the study.

Session Format

Every group is different. These session plans have been designed to give you flexibility and choices. A variety of activities and discussion questions are included. As you plan each session, keep the session goals in mind and select the activities and discussion questions that will be most meaningful for your group.

Read the section titled "Before the Session" several days in advance of your meeting time. A few activities suggest making some preparations in advance.

In many cases, your session time will be too short to do everything that is suggested here. Select activities and questions that best fit the personality of the group ahead of time. Decide how much time you want to allow for each part of the session plan.

Each session plan follows this outline.

Planning the Session

Session Goals
Biblical Foundation
Before the Session

Getting Started

Opening Activities
Leading into the Study
Opening Prayer

Learning Together

Video Study and Discussion
Bible Study and Discussion
Book Study and Discussion
Optional Activity

Wrapping Up

Closing Activity
Closing Prayer

Preparing for the Session

- Pray for the leading of the Holy Spirit as you prepare for the study. Pray for discernment for yourself and for each member of the study group.
- Before each session, familiarize yourself with the content. Read the book chapter again and watch the video segment. Read the scripture passages that support each lesson. Feel free to consult different translations.
- Read through the lesson plan, then go back and choose the activities and questions you wish to use during the session. Plan carefully, yet also be prepared to adjust the session as group members interact and questions arise. Allow space for the Holy Spirit to move in and through the material, the group members, and you as facilitator.
- Secure in advance a TV and DVD player or a computer with projection.
- Prepare the space so that it will enhance the learning process. Ideally, group members should be seated around a table or in a circle so that all can see one another. Movable chairs are best so participants may easily form pairs or small groups for discussion.
- Bring a supply of Bibles for those who forget to bring their own. It is helpful to have a variety of translations.
- For each session you will also need a whiteboard and markers, a chalkboard and chalk, or an easel with paper and markers.

Shaping the Learning Environment

- Begin and end on time.
- Create a climate of openness, encouraging group members to participate as they feel comfortable. Remember that some people will jump right in with answers and comments, while others will need time to process what is being discussed.
- If you notice that some group members don't enter the conversation, ask them if they have thoughts to share. Give everyone a chance

to talk, but keep the conversation moving. Try to prevent a few individuals from doing all the talking.

- Communicate the importance of group discussions and group activities.

- If no one answers at first during discussions, don't be afraid of pauses. Count silently to ten; then say something such as "Would anyone like to go first?" If no one responds, venture an answer yourself and ask for comments.

- Model openness as you share with the group. Group members will follow your example. If you limit your sharing to a surface level, others will follow suit.

- Encourage multiple answers or responses before moving on.

- Ask "Why?" or "Why do you believe that?" or "Can you say more about that?" to help continue a discussion and give it greater depth.

- Affirm others' responses with comments such as "Great" or "Thanks" or "Good insight."

- Monitor your own contributions. If you find yourself doing most of the talking, back off so that you don't train the group to listen rather than speak up.

- Remember that you don't have all the answers. Your job is to keep the discussion going and encourage participation.

- Honor the time schedule. If a session is running longer than expected, get consensus from the group before continuing beyond the agreed-upon ending time.

- Involve group members in various aspects of the group session, such as playing the DVD, saying prayers, or reading the Scripture.

- Note that the session plans sometimes call for breaking into smaller groups. This gives everyone a chance to speak and participate fully. Mix up the teams; don't let the same people pair up on every activity.

- Confidentiality is essential because some discussions and activities call for personal sharing. Let group members know that they should never pass along stories that have been shared in the group. At the beginning of each session remind the group members that confidentiality is crucial to the success of this study.

Tips for Online Meetings

Meeting online is a great option for a number of situations. When circumstances preclude meeting in person, online meetings are a welcome opportunity for people to converse while seeing one another's faces. Online meetings can also expand the "neighborhood" of possible group members, because people can log in from just about anywhere in the world. This also gives those who do not have access to transportation or who prefer not to travel at certain times of day the chance to participate.

One popular option is Zoom. This platform is used quite a bit by businesses. If your church has an account, this can be a good medium. Google Meet, Webex, and Microsoft Teams are other good choices. Individuals can obtain free accounts for each of these platforms, but there may be restrictions (for instance, Zoom's free version limits meetings to forty minutes). Check each platform's website to be sure you are aware of any such restrictions before you sign up.

Video Sharing

For a video-based study, it's important to be able to screen-share your videos so that all participants can view them in your study session. The good news is, whether you have the videos on DVD or streaming files, it is possible to play them in your session.

- All of the videoconferencing platforms mentioned above support screen-sharing videos. Some have specific requirements for assuring that sound will play clearly along with the videos. Follow your videoconferencing platform instructions carefully, and test the video sharing in advance to be sure it works.
- If you wish to screen-share a DVD video, you may need to use a different media player. Some media players will not allow you to share your screen when you play copyright-protected DVDs. VLC is a free media player that is safe and easy to use. To try this software, download at videolan.org/VLC.
- *What about copyright?* DVDs like those you use for group study are meant to be used in a group setting in "real time." That is, whether

11

you meet in person, online, or in a hybrid setting, Abingdon Press encourages use of your DVD or streaming video.

- *What is allowed:* Streaming an Abingdon DVD over Zoom, Teams, or similar platform during a small group session.
- *What is not allowed:* Posting video of a published DVD study to social media or YouTube for later viewing.
- If you have any questions about permissions and copyright, email permissions@abingdonpress.com.
- The streaming subscription platform Amplify Media makes it easy to share streaming videos for groups. When your church has an Amplify subscription, your group members can sign on and have access to the video sessions.
- Visit AmplifyMedia.com to learn more.

Training and Practice

- Choose a platform and practice using it, so you are comfortable with it. Engage in a couple of practice runs with another person.
- Set up a training meeting.
- In advance, teach participants how to log in. Tell them that you will send them an invitation via email, and that it will include a link for them to click at the time of the meeting.
- For those who do not have internet service, let them know they may telephone into the meeting. Provide them the number and let them know that there is usually a unique phone number for each meeting.
- During the training meeting, show them the basic tools available for them to use. They can learn other tools as they feel more confident.

During the Meetings

- **Early invitations.** Send out invitations at least a week in advance. Many meeting platforms enable you to do this through their software.
- **Early log in.** Participants should log in at least ten minutes in advance, to test their audio and their video connections.

- **Talking/not talking.** Instruct participants to keep their microphones muted during the meeting, so extraneous noise from their location does not interrupt the meeting. This includes chewing or yawning sounds, which can be embarrassing! When it is time for discussion, participants can unmute themselves. However, ask them to raise their hand or wave when they are ready to share, so you can call on them. Give folks a few minutes to speak up. They may not be used to conversing in web conferences.

SESSION 1
FINDING GRACE

Planning the Session

Session Goals

Through conversation, activities, and reflection, participants will:

- discover the early history of Methodism;
- explore the meaning of grace, including the difference between prevenient grace, justifying grace, and sanctifying grace; and
- reflect on the ways they have and have not accepted God's gift of grace.

Biblical Foundation

- Ephesians 2:8-9

Before the Session

- Set up a table in the room with name tags, markers, Bibles, extra copies of *Knowing Who We Are,* and paper and pencils.
- Prepare a sign-in sheet with space for each participant to write his or her name and contact information.

- Write the author's three general goals of the study as listed under "Leading into the Study" on a board or large piece of chart paper and display them in a prominent place in the room during the study.
- Write the heading "Salvation" on a board or chart paper. Leave room below the heading to record group responses during the Book Study and Discussion.
- Write the heading "Grace" on a board or chart paper with three subheadings: Prevenient, Justifying, and Sanctifying. Leave room under the three subheadings for group responses during the Book Study and Discussion.
- Have a whiteboard and markers, a chalkboard and chalk, or chart paper and markers available for use during the session.
- Read the Optional Activity and make preparations if you would like to include this in your lesson plan.

Getting Started

Opening Activities

Greet participants as they arrive. Invite them to make a name tag and also pick up a Bible and/or copy of *Knowing Who We Are* if they do not have these.

Welcome participants. Introduce yourself and share why you are excited to be facilitating this study of the book *Knowing Who We Are*.

Invite participants to introduce themselves and share a sentence or two about why they are interested in this study of the book *Knowing Who We Are*.

Housekeeping

- Share any necessary information about your meeting space, parking, and the course schedule.
- Collect contact information from each participant in case you need to share information during the course, and also share your contact information with participants.
- Let participants know you will be faithful to the time and encourage everyone to arrive on time.

- Encourage participants to read the upcoming chapter before the next session.
- You may want to invite participants to have a notebook, journal, or electronic tablet for use during this study. Explain that these can be used to record questions and insights they have as they read each chapter and to take notes during each session.
- Ask participants to covenant together to respect a policy of confidentiality within the group.

Leading into the Study

Read this paragraph from the introduction of *Knowing Who We Are*:

The purpose of this book is to offer those involved in church life a deeper understanding of the distinctives of Methodism to strengthen our sense of identity, better express our beliefs, and deepen our connections within The United Methodist Church. This study engages a set of important values and characteristics that make Wesleyan/Methodist Christianity distinctive— such as God's grace for all and sanctification as tangible transformation in individuals, communities, and creation.

Highlight the three general goals of this study as stated in this paragraph:

1. strengthen our sense of identity,
2. better express our beliefs, and
3. deepen our connections within The United Methodist Church.

Offer a brief overview of the chapters using the section titled "Description of Chapters" as a guide.

Opening Prayer

Holy and loving God, thank you for this time when we may gather to study your holy word. Guide us as we seek to grow in our understanding of The United Methodist Church and what it means for us to follow Christ and share your love and grace with the world. Let us be mindful of your Holy Spirit moving among us, drawing us closer to you, and strengthening our friendships with one another. In the name of your Son, Jesus Christ, we pray. Amen.

Learning Together

Video Study and Discussion

Play the video for Session 1. Discuss:

* Did anything specific stand out as you watched the video?
* What is something you learned or experienced that seems new or *renewed*?

Invite the group to keep both the video and the book in mind throughout the discussion below.

Bible Study and Discussion: Ephesians 2:8-9

"What is Grace?"

Read Ephesians 2:8-9 or invite a volunteer to read this passage. It is printed in chapter 1 under the section title "What Is Grace?"

> *"For by grace you have been saved through faith, and this is not your own doing;*
> *it is the gift of God—not the result of works, so that no one may boast."*
>
> (Ephesians 2:8-9)

Refer to the section of chapter 1 titled "What Is Grace?" during the discussion of the following questions. (There will be a time for discussion of prevenient, justifying, and sanctifying grace later in the session.)
Ask:

* What words might we use to describe grace? (*Responses may include: gift, free, loving, forgiving, undeserved, healing, reconciling, transforming.*)
* How do you respond to the truth that you are saved "by grace" and "not the result of works" as Ephesians 2:8-9 states?
* How easy or difficult is it for you to accept that salvation is a free, unmerited gift of grace?

Close the Bible Study and Discussion by reading Ephesians 2:8-9 again.

Book Study and Discussion

History

Share these key points about the early Methodist movement as noted in the opening section of chapter 1, "Finding Grace":

- "Within Christianity, and Methodism specifically, the doctrine of grace is the central theme of God's relationship to humanity."
- The story of early Methodism "is characterized by searching for and finding grace."
- The Methodist beliefs about grace are grounded in Scripture.
- Methodism began as a renewal movement within the Church of England.
- A quote from John Wesley: "What may we reasonably believe to be God's design in raising up the Preachers called Methodists? A. To reform the nation and, in particular, the Church; to spread scriptural holiness over the land."

The sections in chapter 1 titled "Where Are We From?" and "Methodism's Story: Finding Grace" contain historical information about the Church of England and the Wesley family. Using these two sections as a guide, offer information about these key points:

- Elizabeth I and the Act of Uniformity (1559),
- The life of Susanna and Samuel Wesley,
- John and Charles Wesley remained ordained ministers in the Church of England,
- John Wesley's pamphlet "Short History of Methodism" and his description of the "Three Rises of Methodism":
  - ◊ 1st Rise—College students in Oxford and the formation of small groups,
  - ◊ 2nd Rise—John and Charles's experiences in Georgia, and
  - ◊ 3rd Rise—John and Charles's experiences in London after their return from Georgia. Of major significance here are (1) John's acquaintance with the Moravians and Peter Bohler and (2) Charles and John's experiences of assurance.

Ask:

- Why is it significant that Methodism began as a renewal movement as opposed to a movement in response to a theological or other conflict?
- In what ways do you identify with Charles and John's search for renewal, grace, and assurance?

Share the author's statement, "Significant threads from our origin story include an earnest search for God's grace, accepting God's grace, taking risks to learn more about and organize to share God's grace in mission."

Note that Methodism is unique because it is missional. The Latin root *missio* means sent or sending.

Read John 20:19-22.

Salvation

Instruct participants to refer to the sections titled "From Grace to Good Works: What Is Salvation?" and "Salvation Now…and Not Yet" as they respond to the following questions. Write responses on a board or large piece of chart paper to provide a visual word picture of the various aspects of salvation.

Ask:

- What is salvation?
- What does it mean to have salvation both now and not yet?

Read the last paragraph of the section titled "Salvation Now…and Not Yet" as it is printed below. This paragraph offers a step-by-step description of our experience of salvation. Pause after you read each sentence and offer time for reflection, discussion, and questions.

- "John Wesley describes salvation as available now.
- Living into the wholeness of God's salvation in Jesus Christ through the Holy Spirit for us through grace alone changes everything.
- When we receive God's grace, we experience salvation, not only the ultimate wholeness of union with the Triune God, but the assurance now of reconciled relationships with God and others.

- Through our baptism we are initiated into the body of Christ and commissioned to love God and neighbor in our words and lives.
- This new identity as children of God gives us purpose and peace in the midst of a troubled world as we participate in God's unfolding work."

Grace

Share this quote, "Accepting and relying on God's grace for salvation is the most important component of Christian faith."

Call attention to John Wesley's three categories of grace: prevenient, justifying, and sanctifying. Note that the author offers multiple descriptions and examples of each category of grace. Encourage participants to refer to the text and explore these as they discuss the following questions. Record group responses in the appropriate column on the board or chart paper with the heading "Grace."

Ask:

- What is prevenient grace?
- How have you experienced prevenient grace in your life?

Share these sentences from the section "Prevenient Grace" during the discussion:

- "God's prevenient grace precedes our awareness, leading us toward God and one another for the purpose of receiving God's grace and salvation."
- "Prevenient grace means the grace that 'comes before.'"
- "One essential purpose of grace, initiated by prevenient grace, is to restore the image of God, God's goodness, in persons."

Ask:

- What is justifying grace?

- How is justifying grace connected to/related to baptism?
- How have you accepted or experienced justifying grace in your life?

Share this quote from "Justifying Grace" during this discussion:

In response to justifying grace, one repents of sin and receives an assurance of one's salvation. For United Methodists drawing on Scripture and John Wesley, justification most often occurs as an event, not a process. At justification the process of sanctification begins.

Invite a volunteer to read aloud the section titled "Sanctifying Grace." Share this quote from the section "Good Works: Growing in Holiness":

Holiness is the reflection of God's image and love in our lives.... Holiness is God's work in us. We do not seek to earn God's grace anxiously worrying about our worthiness. Accepting God's grace in Jesus Christ and receiving the Holy Spirit opens us to following the example of Jesus and growing in holiness.

Ask:

- When have you or do you engage in good works in an effort to earn God's love, grace, and salvation?
- When has your engagement in good works been in response to God's free gifts of love, grace, and salvation?

Optional Activity—Holy Tenacity

Call attention to the section of the introduction titled "Holy Tenacity: Methodism's Story" and highlight key points.

Remind the group that Methodism is unique because it is missional. We believe we are sent in the name of Christ to share God's love with the world. Ask:

- How do we as the church and as individuals practice holy tenacity in response to the call to be missional in our communities and our world today?

Wrapping Up

Closing Activity

Invite participants to reflect for a minute on the information presented in the introduction and chapter 1 of *Knowing Who We Are*.

Then invite discussion of this question:

- How has your understanding of Methodism been broadened or strengthened?

Closing Prayer

Loving God, thank you for your gifts of love, grace, and salvation. Thank you for your grace that goes before us and draws us to you. Thank you for your grace that forgives us and calls us righteous. Thank you for your grace that helps us grow in holiness. Guide and strengthen us as we willingly and joyfully follow the example of Christ and share your love with the world. Amen.

SESSION 2
SAVING SMALL GROUPS

Planning the Session

Session Goals

Through conversation, activities, and reflection, participants will:

- explore the integration of doctrine and practice (focus of Bible Study and Discussion),
- understand the purpose and benefits of small groups both in the time of John Wesley and today, and
- resolve to follow John Wesley's General Rules.

Biblical Foundation

- Ephesians 4:32
- Colossians 3:12

Before the Session

- Set up a table in the room with name tags, markers, Bibles, extra copies of *Knowing Who We Are*, and paper and pencils. Also set out the sign-in sheet for newcomers.

- Write the heading "To Watch over One Another in Love" on a board or chart paper. This will be used during the Bible Study and Discussion.
- Write the heading "Characteristics of Wesley's Small Groups" on a board or chart paper. This will be used during the Book Study and Discussion.
- Have a whiteboard and markers, a chalkboard and chalk, or chart paper and markers available for use during the session.
- Read the Optional Activity and make preparations if you would like to include this in your lesson plan.

Getting Started

Opening Activities

Greet participants as they arrive. Invite them to make a name tag and also pick up a Bible and/or copy of *Knowing Who We Are* if they do not have these.

Welcome participants. If there are newcomers offer a short time for introductions.

Share any necessary housekeeping information from the list in Session 1. Remind the group to respect a policy of confidentiality.

Leading into the Study

Remind the group of the purpose of this study by reading this paragraph from the introduction of *Knowing Who We Are*:

The purpose of this book is to offer those involved in church life a deeper understanding of the distinctives of Methodism to strengthen our sense of identity, better express our beliefs, and deepen our connections within The United Methodist Church. This study engages a set of important values and characteristics that make Wesleyan/Methodist Christianity distinctive— such as God's grace for all and sanctification as tangible transformation in individuals, communities, and creation.

Call attention to the title of chapter 2, "Saving Small Groups." Note that this title may be interpreted two ways:

- Small groups in our churches are worth saving.
- Small groups offer individuals an opportunity to be saved, to know and accept the saving power of Christ.

Invite discussion of these questions:

- In what small groups have you participated?
- How were these small groups beneficial for you?
- Were any of these small groups harmful for you, and if so, in what ways?
- Have you felt unwelcome in a group that seemed to be exclusive?
- What are the characteristics of a welcoming and inclusive group?

Note that John Wesley and the early Methodists wanted to be inclusive and were called "friends to all."

Opening Prayer

Holy and loving God, thank you for John and Charles Wesley and the other men and women of faith who accepted your call to proclaim the love of Christ and make disciples. Thank you for this small group and this opportunity to study, learn, and grow together. Help us to continue to grow in faith and love so that we may be faithful witnesses of your love and grace in the world. In the name of your Son, Jesus Christ, we pray. Amen.

Learning Together

Video Study and Discussion

Play the video for Session 2. Discuss:

- Did anything specific stand out as you watched the video?
- What is something you learned or experienced that seems new or *renewed*?

Invite the group to keep both the video and the book in mind throughout the discussion.

Bible Study and Discussion:
Ephesians 4:32 and Colossians 3:12

"To Watch over One Another in Love"

Share this quote from the section titled "To Watch Over One Another in Love":

> The early Methodist movement's distinctiveness was not in its innovation, but in a powerfully simple integration of doctrine and practice moving us toward a faithful embodiment of Christlikeness.

Explain that the purpose of this Bible Study and Discussion is to explore how the "integration of doctrine and practice" teaches us how "To Watch over One Another in Love."

During the discussion of Ephesians 4:32 and Colossians 3:12, write the "practices" on the board or chart paper under the heading "To Watch over One Another in Love."

Read Ephesians 4:32: "Be kind to one another, tenderhearted, forgiving one another, as God in Christ has forgiven you."

Ask:

- What is the doctrine or theological truth revealed in this Bible verse? (*God, through Christ, has forgiven us.*)
- How are we called to respond to this theological truth in practice, that is, in the way we live our lives? (*By extending kindness, compassion, and forgiveness to others as God extends these to us.*)
- What challenges do you face in the practice of kindness, compassion, and forgiveness toward others?
- How have you experienced the Lord's kindness, compassion, and forgiveness through the actions of others?

Read Colossians 3:12: "Therefore, as God's chosen ones, holy and beloved, clothe yourselves with compassion, kindness, humility, meekness, and patience."

Ask:

- What is the doctrine or theological truth revealed in this Bible verse? (*God has chosen us, loves us, and makes us holy.*)
- How are we called to respond to this theological truth in practice, that is, in the way we live our lives? ("*clothe yourself with compassion, kindness, humility, meekness, and patience*")
- Which of these five attributes are easy for you to practice?
- Which of these five attributes present challenges for you?

Read Ephesians 4:32 and Colossians 3:12 again. Ask:

- How does John Wesley's distinctive method of integrating doctrine and practice raise up faithful followers who are powerful witnesses for Christ?
- How does John Wesley's distinctive method of integrating doctrine and practice help us grow to be more like Christ and "watch over one another in love"?

Book Study and Discussion

Recruit a volunteer to be the scribe during the session. Instruct the scribe to list characteristics of Wesley's small groups as these are mentioned during the discussion. The list may include the types and purposes of different small groups, benefits and results, and the number of people attending.

Note that John Wesley organized a variety of small groups that fulfilled different purposes. These included trial groups, penitent groups, select societies, and general bands.

Instruct participants to refer to the section "A Different Kind of Small Group?" as they respond to the following questions. Ask:

- What was the only requirement for a person who wanted to participate in a "trial band," which was the first small group? (*a desire for salvation*)
- What are the three General Rules the disciples needed to follow in order to remain in the trial band? (*to do no harm, to do good and avoid evil, to attend to the ordinances of God*)

- What was the purpose of the "penitent bands"? (*nurture*)

Explain that when participants were ready to leave a penitent band, they would participate in either:

- select societies that provided both nurture and mentors for leaders or
- general bands where people with similar characteristics were grouped together.

Invite a volunteer to read the last paragraph of the section "A Different Kind of Small Group?"

Ask:

- What small groups in our churches today fulfill the purposes of the small groups formed by John Wesley?
- Are people today open to being in groups that hold one another accountable?

The section titled "Counting Conversion" offers a summary of the beginning of Methodism through field preaching and small groups or societies.

Share a summary of this section highlighting:

- the first field preachers in the Methodist movement, including George Whitefield, John Wesley, and Charles Wesley;
- the development and impact of small groups/societies; and
- John Wesley's experiment regarding effectiveness of small groups. He concluded the small groups were effective because they provided what preaching alone could not. John Wesley was quoted to say, "The preacher had little opportunity for instructions, the awakened souls could not 'watch over one another in love,' and the believers could not 'build up one another and bear one another's burdens.'"

Call attention to the first sentence under "Counting Conversion" and note the observation that early Methodism was more focused on helping people grow in grace and less focused on numbers.

Ask:

- Where is the focus of Methodism today?

In the section titled "Comfortably Slack," the author notes that John Wesley emphasized a "middle way" between the extreme and opposing views of Roman Catholics and Puritans regarding faith and works.

Review the meaning of prevenient grace, justifying grace, and sanctifying grace from Session 1. Then ask:

- How do justifying grace and sanctifying grace describe John Wesley's understanding of the relationship between faith and works? (Note the author's explanation that first, "human beings are justified by faith alone in Jesus Christ" and then "sanctified by the Holy Spirit that empowers human beings to engage in practices that shape a life of holiness." John Wesley believed that faith comes first, and works are done in response to faith.)
- How do you understand the relationship between faith and works in your own life?
- How do you respond to the idea that "comfortably slack" describes religion in mainstream America?

Invite a volunteer to read the first paragraph in the section "To Watch Over One Another in Love."

Note that Wesley believed it was important to have connection among Methodist Christians for (1) "mutual support and accountability" and (2) "forming believers in holiness of heart and life."

Highlight John Wesley's three general rules, as described by Bishop Rueben Job in *Three Simple Rules: A Wesleyan Way of Living* (Nashville: Abingdon, 2007, 19, 33, and 51):

- Do No Harm—"By doing no harm, by avoiding evil of every kind, especially that which is most generally practiced."
- Do Good—"By doing good; by being in every kind merciful after their power; as they have opportunity, doing good of every possible sort, and, as far as possible, to all..."

- Stay in Love With God—"By attending upon all the ordinances of God...."

Ask:

- How do these three General Rules provide a guide for the church today as we seek to stay connected through "mutual support and accountability"?
- How does the daily practice of these three General Rules form "believers in holiness of heart and life"?

The Optional Activity focuses on the third General Rule and "the ordinances of God."

Optional Activity—Means of Grace

Read the third General Rule: Stay in Love With God—"By attending upon all the ordinances of God.... "

Share these key points:

- The "ordinances of God" are spiritual disciplines or practices, also known as "Means of Grace."
- "John Wesley and others made a distinction between works of piety and works of charity."
- Spiritual Disciplines or Means of Grace may be practiced both individually and in community with others.
- Works of Piety include: "worship, prayer, praying the psalms, singing, Bible study, fasting."
- Works of Charity include "feeding the hungry, caring for the poor, working for justice/reform."

Ask:

- What individual spiritual disciplines/practices/ordinances do you find meaningful?
- What spiritual disciplines/practices/ordinances do you find meaningful in community with others?

- How has your participation in works of piety and charity been a means of grace for you?

You may continue this Optional Activity by leading the group in a spiritual practice together, for example, praying a psalm, *Lectio Divina*, or singing a hymn.

Wrapping Up

Closing Activity

Read the conclusion to chapter 2 of *Knowing Who We Are*.
Remind the group of the topics discussed in this session:

- integration of doctrine and practice,
- benefits of small groups,
- Wesley's Three General Rules, and
- spiritual practices

Ask:

- Moving forward, what actions would you like to take that will help you continue to grow in "holiness of heart and life"? (If time is short suggest that participants think about this question during the coming week.)

Closing Prayer

Holy Lord, open our hearts to receive your grace that we may grow in holiness of heart and live holy lives following the example of Christ. Give us the discipline to practice works of piety and charity so that we may remain mindful of your grace and open to the work of the Holy Spirit in our lives. In the name of your Son, Jesus Christ, we pray. Amen.

SESSION 3
LOCAL AND CONNECTIONAL

Planning the Session

Session Goals

Through conversation, activities, and reflection, participants will:

- affirm the local church as "the primary place for preaching and worship";
- understand the connectional nature of The United Methodist Church; and
- reflect on their own experiences of Holy Communion, Baptism, Confirmation, and worship.

Biblical Foundation

- Matthew 26:26-30

Before the Session

- Set up a table in the room with name tags, markers, Bibles, extra copies of *Knowing Who We Are*, paper and pencils, and the sign-in sheet.

- Write the heading "Local Church" on a board or chart paper. This will be used during the Leading into the Study conversation.
- Have a whiteboard and markers, a chalkboard and chalk, or chart paper and markers available for use during the session.
- Read the Optional Activities and decide if you want to include any of these in your lesson plan. The Optional Activities provide an opportunity for participants to become more familiar with the hymns and liturgies for worship in *The United Methodist Hymnal*. The activities are numbered and you will find suggestions within the session plan as to where to include each activity. You will need a supply of *The United Methodist Hymnals*, enough for each person to have one.

Getting Started

Opening Activities

Greet participants as they arrive. Invite them to make a name tag and pick up a Bible and/or copy of *Knowing Who We Are* if they do not have these.

Welcome participants and offer a time for introductions if there are newcomers.

Share any necessary information from the housekeeping list in Session 1. Remind the group to covenant together to respect a policy of confidentiality.

If you plan to do any of the Optional Activities, distribute *The United Methodist Hymnals* to the group.

Leading into the Study

Remind the group of the purpose of this study by reading this paragraph from the introduction of *Knowing Who We Are*:

The purpose of this book is to offer those involved in church life a deeper understanding of the distinctives of Methodism to strengthen our sense of identity, better express our beliefs, and deepen our connections within The United Methodist Church. This study engages a set of important values and characteristics that make Wesleyan/Methodist Christianity distinctive—

such as God's grace for all and sanctification as tangible transformation in individuals, communities, and creation.

Call attention to the board or paper with the heading "Local Church."

Recruit a volunteer to serve as scribe and record responses from the group under the heading.

Instruct participants to refer to the section of chapter 3 titled "Local Church" as they respond to these questions. This section includes statements related to the purpose and mission of the local church. You may only need to ask one or two of these questions to keep the conversation going. Ask:

- What is a local church?
- Why does a local church exist?
- What activities take place in a local church?
- What purposes and/or activities have you experienced in a local church that are not mentioned in this section of *Knowing Who We Are*?

Opening Prayer

Holy and loving God, we thank you for the fellowship of the church. We thank you for this body of believers with whom we may worship, grow in faith, and serve you. Help us to be mindful of people who do not participate in the life of a local church. Open our eyes and our hearts to the ways we may welcome them into the fellowship of the church. In the name of your Son, Jesus Christ, we pray. Amen.

Learning Together

Video Study and Discussion

Play the video for Session 3. Discuss:

- Did anything specific stand out as you watched the video?
- What is something you learned or experienced that seems new or *renewed*?

Invite the group to keep both the video and the book in mind throughout the discussion below.

Bible Study and Discussion: Matthew 26:26-30

The Last Supper

Read the account of the Last Supper recorded in Matthew 26:26-30. Invite discussion of these questions:

- What does Jesus do and say in this story?
- How does Jesus connect past, present, and future in the sharing of the bread and cup? (*The phrase "blood of the covenant" connects Jesus's actions with God's covenant with the Israelites, which was sealed with blood [see Exodus 24:3-8]. Jesus looks ahead to "my Father's kingdom." The apostle Paul described the church as the body of Christ.*)
- How does your participation in the Lord's Supper help you feel connected to the past, present, and future? (*Responses may include: connection with the biblical story and believers throughout history, fellowship with believers gathered around the Communion Table, looking ahead to eternal life.*)
- Jesus shared this meal in a private setting with only a few who were closest to him. How did Jesus indicate the far-reaching and inclusive nature of his purpose as symbolized in the bread and cup? (*Jesus gave his body and blood "for many for the forgiveness of sins."*)

You may want to do Optional Activity #1, Services of Word and Table, here.

Book Study and Discussion

Share these key points from the section titled "Worship":

- Our worship practices connect us to the worship practices of God's people in the Old Testament, to Jesus leading worship with his disciples, and to previous generations of God's people who have worshipped before us.

- Our worship experiences have three main components: hearing the Word, responding to the Word, and Holy Communion.

Invite discussion of the following questions:

- How do we hear the Word proclaimed when we gather to worship? (*Responses may include sermons, Scripture readings, hymn-singing, and various forms of the arts including music, liturgical dance, visual arts.*)
- How do we respond to the Word proclaimed when we gather to worship? (*Answers may include reciting a creed; praying; praising; offering gifts of money, talents, and service.*)
- In what ways do you feel connected to the biblical story and previous generations when you worship? (*Responses may include reciting Old Testament psalms of prayer and praise, partaking of Holy Communion, singing a grandparent's favorite hymn, remembering worshipping as a child as you take children to worship.*)

Highlight these key points from "A Singing People":

- Methodists have been "a singing people" since the beginning of the Wesleys' renewal movement,
- Charles Wesley's hymns include words and images from Scripture, and
- We learn Methodist doctrine from Wesley's hymns.

Offer time for participants to share the titles of hymns and spiritual songs that are special to them and why.

You may want to ask these questions during the discussion:

- What hymns have helped you through times of crisis?
- What hymns are comforting to you?
- What hymns have helped you grow in faith and understanding of Scripture?
- What hymns have helped you express your praise, adoration, and thanksgiving?

You may want to include Optional Activity #2, The Hymns of Charles Wesley, here.

Invite a volunteer to read the first paragraph of the section "Baptism: By Water and the Spirit."

Explain that baptized believers may participate in the ritual of Confirmation and become a member of The United Methodist Church.

Invite the group to read the Confirmation vows together as printed in *Knowing Who We Are.*

Ask:

- Why do United Methodists not rebaptize a person who has been baptized?
- Have you participated in a reaffirmation of your baptism? If so, what was that experience like for you?

You may want to do Optional Activity #3 (below), The Baptismal Covenant, here.

Summarize the information in the section "Conference as Connection."

Invite discussion of the ways this structure of conferences, from local charge conferences to the global General Conference, connects United Methodists with one another all over the globe.

Invite group members who have participated in their local church charge conference, a session of annual conference, or a jurisdictional or General Conference to share their experiences.

Call attention to the various councils and agencies mentioned in the section "Structured for Service."

Ask:

- What are the different areas of ministry represented by these councils and agencies? (You may want to list them on a board or chart paper.)

Optional Activities—*The United Methodist Hymnal*

Each participant will need a copy of *The United Methodist Hymnal* for these activities. It will also work for two people to share a hymnal.

Activity 1: Services of Word and Table

You may include this activity as part of the Bible Study and Discussion.

Note that *The United Methodist Hymnal* contains four services of Word and Table:

- An order for worship including the sermon and Holy Communion.
- An order for worship that begins with the Invitation for Holy Communion.
- An order for worship that includes only the congregational responses.
- A traditional ritual from the former Methodist and former Evangelical United Brethren churches.

Instruct participants to find A Service of Word and Table II and A Service of Word and Table IV in the beginning of the hymnal.

Invite participants to read the Invitation and the Confession and Pardon from A Service of Word and Table II together. Then invite participants to read the Invitation and the Confession and Pardon for A Service of Word and Table IV together.

Ask:

- Are you more familiar with the liturgy for Service II or Service IV?
- Has your congregation used any of the musical settings?
- What parts of the liturgy for Holy Communion do you find most meaningful?

Activity 2: The Hymns of Charles Wesley

Call attention to the several indexes in the back of *The United Methodist Hymnal*.

Instruct participants to find the "Index of Composers, Arrangers, Authors, Translators, and Sources" and then locate the name Charles Wesley.

Offer time for the group to look up several hymns by Charles Wesley. Ask:

- Is this hymn based on a specific Scripture text?
- What does this hymn teach us about our faith?

Activity 3: The Baptismal Covenant

Four services of The Baptismal Covenant are found near the beginning of *The United Methodist Hymnal*. Invite participants to refer to each service in turn. For each service:

- Read the explanation below the title that describes when the service may be celebrated.
- Invite a volunteer to read the "Introduction to the Service."
- Together read the congregational response of welcome.

Ask:

- Why is it important for the congregation to participate by welcoming the ones who have been newly baptized and/or confirmed as members?
- You may want to offer time for participants to share experiences of their own baptisms and/or confirmations.

Wrapping Up

Closing Activity

Read the conclusion to chapter 3 of *Knowing Who We Are*.

Closing Prayer

Holy and loving Lord, thank you for Jesus Christ who died for the sins of the world and rose again so that we may live forever with you. Thank you for the church, for our local church, and for our connection with churches all over the world. Help us to be faithful witnesses and invite others to be part of the body of believers. In the name of your Son, Jesus Christ, we pray. Amen.

SESSION 4
TENACIOUS MISSION

Planning the Session

Session Goals

Through conversation, activities, and reflection, participants will:

* understand what John Wesley meant by "Social Holiness,"
* explore the meaning and impact of "Tenacious Mission," and
* discern how we may be involved in continuing the Methodist tradition of social holiness and tenacious mission.

Biblical Foundation

* 1 Timothy 6:17-19
* 1 John 3:17

Before the Session

* Set up a table in the room with name tags, markers, Bibles, extra copies of *Knowing Who We Are*, paper and pencils, and the sign-in sheet.
* On a board or chart paper draw two vertical lines to create three columns. Write the headings "The Holy Club," "The New Room,"

and "The Foundery" in the three columns along with the years these places were involved in active ministry, noted in the Book Study and Discussion.

- Have a whiteboard and markers, a chalkboard and chalk, or chart paper and markers available for use during the session.
- Read the Optional Activity and decide if you want to include it in your session plan. If so, have chart paper and markers available, along with a few Methodist history books and dictionaries.

Getting Started

Opening Activities

Greet participants as they arrive. Invite them to make a name tag and pick up a Bible and/or copy of *Knowing Who We Are* if they do not have these.

Welcome participants and offer a time for introductions if there are newcomers.

Share any necessary information from the housekeeping list in Session 1. Remind the group to covenant together to respect a policy of confidentiality.

Leading into the Study

Remind the group of the purpose of this study by reading this paragraph from the introduction of *Knowing Who We Are*:

The purpose of this book is to offer those involved in church life a deeper understanding of the distinctives of Methodism to strengthen our sense of identity, better express our beliefs, and deepen our connections within The United Methodist Church. This study engages a set of important values and characteristics that make Wesleyan/Methodist Christianity distinctive— such as God's grace for all and sanctification as tangible transformation in individuals, communities, and creation.

Instruct the group to turn to the opening section of chapter 4. Invite a volunteer to read the second paragraph.

Ask:

- What phrases and ideas in this paragraph stand out for you? (You may want to write the phrases and ideas on a board or chart paper.)
- What contributed to the missional character of Methodism? (*emphasis on nurturing relationships, an interest in the connection between the inner spiritual life and Christian practices of loving our neighbors*)
- What does the word *tenacious* mean? (*persistent, determined, resolute*)

Opening Prayer

Holy and loving God, thank you for the early Methodists who worshipped, studied, served, and grew in faith together. Thank you for the foundation they built for us and the example they gave us of how to follow you. Open our hearts and minds so that we may learn from them and continue the work of tenacious mission, as we share the gospel and minister to the needs of others. In the name of your Son, Jesus Christ, we pray. Amen.

Learning Together

Video Study and Discussion

Play the video for Session 4. Discuss:

- Did anything specific stand out as you watched the video?
- What is something you learned or experienced that seems new or *renewed*?

Invite the group to keep both the video and the book in mind throughout the discussion below.

Bible Study and Discussion: 1 Timothy 6:17-19; 1 John 3:17

"Give All You Can"

*Note: Before the session, reread the section "'Give All You Can': Early Methodist Practices of Wealth-sharing" and make a note of specific points

related to John Wesley and giving that you would like to highlight as part of the Bible Study and Discussion.

Call attention to the author's statement that:

- the Bible speaks most about love, and
- after love, the Bible speaks most about money and possessions.

Instruct the group to turn to the section of chapter 4 titled "Give All You Can," and find the four cornerstones of John Wesley's teachings about wealth and possessions as suggested by Randy Maddox.

Invite a volunteer to read the four cornerstones:

- the source of all things is God and so all things belong to God,
- earthly wealth has been placed in human hands to be stewarded on God's behalf,
- God expects that we use what we are given to provide for our own necessities and then the necessities of others, and
- to spend our God-given resources on luxuries while others are in need of necessities is to misuse what God has given us.

Read 1 Timothy 6:17-19 (NIV):

Command those who are rich in this present world not to be arrogant nor to put their hope in wealth, which is so uncertain, but to put their hope in God, who richly provides us with everything for our enjoyment. Command them to do good, to be rich in good deeds, and to be generous and willing to share. In this way they will lay up treasure for themselves as a firm foundation for the coming age, so that they may take hold of the life that is truly life.

Invite discussion of these questions:

- What does this Scripture passage tell us not to do? Why?
- What does this Scripture passage tell us to do? Why?
- What is "the life that is truly life"? (*Responses may include following Jesus's example of loving and serving, after Jesus washed his disciples' feet he said we will be happy when we serve others [John 13:17], placing our trust and faith in God, generosity, and sharing.*)

43

Read 1 John 3:17 (NIV):

If anyone has material possessions and sees a brother or sister in need but has no pity on them, how can the love of God be in that person?

Ask:

- How do Wesley's four cornerstones or teachings about wealth and possessions reflect the teaching in 1 Timothy 6:17-19 and 1 John 3:17?
- How are these teachings helpful to you?
- What challenges do these teachings present for you?

Book Study and Discussion

Read the short section titled "Redeeming Relationships: 'No Holiness but Social Holiness.'"

Ask:

- Why does Wesley say "no holiness but social holiness"?
- How have you experienced and participated in "social holiness"?

Call attention to the board or chart paper with these three column headings. Note that these places were significant in the early life of Methodism.

- The Holy Club, Oxford (1729–35)
- The New Room, Bristol (1739–the present)
- The Foundery, London (1739–85)

Recruit a volunteer to serve as scribe and write the group's responses to the following questions in the appropriate column.

Invite participants to refer to the information in chapter 4 as they respond to these questions.

Ask:

- Who participated in the Holy Club?
- How did the Holy Club practice social holiness?
- What ministries were provided at the New Room in Bristol?

- How was the New Room a center for the practice of social holiness?
- How was the Foundery a center for the practice of social holiness?
- How did John Wesley and others engage in tenacious mission from the Foundery?

Review the information listed in the three columns. Note that two areas of ministry in early Methodism were medical care and education. The United Methodist Church continues to be "tenacious" in its work in these areas.

Offer a brief summary of the information in the sections "Primitive Physic: Saving Bodies and Souls" and "Education" and highlight the United Methodist medical centers and schools that are active today. Invite participants who have received care, taken classes, or worked at a United Methodist institution to share their experiences.

Read the first sentence of chapter 4: "United Methodism continues a long and tenacious heritage of missional impact."

Review the meaning of "tenacious."

Call attention to the three sections titled:

- "Methodists and Racial Equality,"
- "Methodists and Gender Equality," and
- "Methodists Advocating for Social Justice."

Highlight the fact that Methodists have advocated for racial and gender equality and social justice since the time of John Wesley.

Ask:

- Where in our local community do people experience racial inequality, gender inequality, and social injustice?
- What might we do to continue Methodism's practice of "Tenacious Mission" and work to address these issues?
- Where does racial inequality, gender inequality, and social injustice exist in our country?
- How might we participate in the work of "Tenacious Mission" to alleviate this suffering in our country?
- Where does racial inequality, gender inequality, and social injustice exist around the globe?

- How might we participate in the work of "Tenacious Mission" to alleviate inequality and injustice around the globe?

(*The United Methodist General Board of Global Ministries and UMCOR are at work in local communities around the globe addressing needs in a variety of areas. Local churches may participate with financial gifts and by serving as volunteers.)

Optional Activity—History

Throughout chapter 4, the author offers historical information about mission and outreach work in Methodism. This Optional Activity provides an opportunity for your group to explore this history in more detail.

It is likely participants will have phones or other devices with internet capability that they may use for research. You may also want to bring in Methodist history books or dictionaries that include this information. Check with your minister and church library for resources.

Create small groups of three to five people.

Assign each group an area of history that the author mentions in chapter 4. Ideas include:

- The Holy Club,
- the New Room,
- the Foundery,
- medical missions,
- education,
- racial and/or gender equality, and
- an area of social justice.

Instruct the small groups to:

- research the information in chapter 4 related to your topic,
- look up additional information using the internet and research books,
- write key points on a piece of chart paper, and
- prepare a short report to share with the whole group.

Also let the small groups know how much time is available for this activity.

When the time is up call the small groups back together to share their findings.

Wrapping Up

Closing Activity

Invite discussion of this quote from the section "Holy Tenacity: Advocacy for God's Work":

"John Wesley's remarks remind me of the importance of taking risks, even uncomfortable ones as we follow Christ's example to love God and neighbor. The Holy Spirit often guides us into unexpected places to serve the world in surprising and powerful ways."

Ask:

- When have you taken risks to follow Christ?
- When have you been guided to unexpected places to serve God in surprising and powerful ways?

Closing Prayer

Holy and loving Lord, from the very beginning you have called your people to serve you. You continue to call us to love our neighbor, to provide medical care, education, food, clothing, and shelter for those in need, to pursue equality and justice for all people, to be persistent in doing good works. Give us courage to be tenacious in serving others and drawing others to you. In the name of your Son, Jesus Christ, we pray. Amen.

SESSION 5
TEXTS THAT SHAPE US

Planning the Session

Session Goals

Through conversation, activities, and reflection, participants will:

- affirm that the Bible is the most important book for Christians,
- consider the ways the Scripture shapes our lives,
- reflect on the content and meaning of:
  - ◊ the Nicene Creed and the Apostles' Creed,
  - ◊ the doctrinal document "The Articles of Religion of the Methodist Church," and
  - ◊ the contemporary document "Our Social Creed."

Biblical Foundation

- 2 Timothy 3:14-17

Before the Session

- Set up a table in the room with name tags, markers, Bibles, extra copies of *Knowing Who We Are*, paper and pencils, and the sign-in sheet.

- Collect enough copies of *The United Methodist Hymnal* for each participant to have one. These will be used in the study of the Nicene Creed (#880) and the Apostles' Creed (#881).
- Arrange for participants to view "The Articles of Religion of the Methodist Church." This document may be found at https://www.umc.org/en/content/articles-of-religion. You may print copies from the website or project the document on a screen from a laptop. There are twenty-five Articles. You may want to select a few ahead of time for the class to consider.
- Arrange for participants to view "Our Social Creed." This creed may be found at https://www.umc.org/en/content/our-social-creed. You may print copies from the website or project the document on a screen from a laptop.
- Have a whiteboard and markers, a chalkboard and chalk, or chart paper and markers available for use during the session.
- Read the Optional Activity and make preparations if you want to include it in your session plan.

Getting Started

Opening Activities

Greet participants as they arrive. Invite them to make a name tag and pick up a Bible and/or copy of *Knowing Who We Are* if they do not have these.

Welcome participants and offer a time for introductions if there are newcomers.

Share any necessary information from the housekeeping list in Session 1. Remind the group to covenant together to respect a policy of confidentiality.

Leading into the Study

Remind the group of the purpose of this study by reading this paragraph from the introduction of *Knowing Who We Are*:

The purpose of this book is to offer those involved in church life a deeper understanding of the distinctives of Methodism to strengthen our sense of identity, better express our beliefs, and deepen our connections within The United Methodist Church. This study engages a set of important values and characteristics that make Wesleyan/Methodist Christianity distinctive—such as God's grace for all and sanctification as tangible transformation in individuals, communities, and creation.

Read the title for this lesson, "Texts That Shape Us." Emphasize the fact that the Bible is the most important text for Christians.

Lead a brief discussion of the following questions as a way to help participants think about their own experiences with the Bible.

- What is the Bible?
- When did you receive your first Bible?
- What is one of your favorite Bible verses or stories?

Opening Prayer

Holy and loving God, thank you for the Bible. Thank you for these holy Scriptures through which you reveal yourself to us. Thank you for the words of instruction, the words of wisdom and guidance, and the words of comfort and assurance you have given to us. Open our hearts and minds so that we may be receptive to your Holy Word. In the name of your Son, Jesus Christ, we pray. Amen.

Learning Together

Video Study and Discussion

Play the video for Session 5. Discuss:

- Did anything specific stand out as you watched the video?
- What is something you learned or experienced that seems new or *renewed*?

Invite the group to keep both the video and the book in mind throughout the discussion below.

Bible Study and Discussion: 2 Timothy 3:14-17

Primarily Scripture: Reading Scripture with Wesley

Read 2 Timothy 3:14-17.
Share these key points:

- The phrase "You know who taught you" refers to Eunice, Timothy's mother, and Lois, Timothy's grandmother.
- The author notes that the word *inspiration* is from the Latin *inspirare*, which means "to breathe life into, animate, excite."
- John Wesley understood that God inspired the writers of Scripture and that God inspires our reading of Scripture.

Ask:

- How have you experienced God's inspiration and presence when you read Scripture?
- How do you see Wesley's theology and practice coinciding with Paul's words in this Scripture? For example:
  ◊ Wesley encouraged his pastors and leaders—verse 14.
  ◊ Wesley believed the primary purpose or "telos" of reading Scripture was salvation—verse 15.
  ◊ Wesley formed small groups for the purposes of "teaching, for showing mistakes, for correcting, and for training character"— verse 16.
  ◊ Wesley believed we respond to God's grace by serving others and doing "everything that is good"—verse 17.

Read this quote from the section "Primarily Scripture: Reading Scripture with Wesley":

O give me the book!...Let me be *homo unius libri* [a person of one book]. Here I am, far from the busy ways of men. I sit down alone: only God is here. In his presence I open, I read his Book; for this end, to find the way to heaven.

51

Ask:

- When do you read the Bible?
- Why do you read the Bible?
- Does this quote from Wesley inspire you and if so, how?

Book Study and Discussion

Invite conversation about the first sentence in the section "What is Scripture?":

John Wesley and the early Methodists understood that Scripture, while inspired and authoritative, was not always clear and transparent in its meaning and influence on the lives of believers.

Invite participants to refer to the sections "What is Scripture?" and "Beginning with God" as they respond to these questions:

- How many books are in the Old Testament?
- What types of literature are found in the Old Testament?
- How many books are in the New Testament?
- What types of literature are found in the New Testament?
- What is the Apocrypha or Deuterocanon?
- Why is it important that the Bible begins with God?
- What are key themes in the Bible?

Draw attention to three key components of "A Wesleyan Way of Reading Scripture."

One—Inspiration of the Holy Spirit

Note that Wesley was aware of the presence of the Holy Spirit in Scripture with both the biblical writers and the ones who read the Scripture.

Highlight the quote from Thomas á Kempis (a German-Dutch priest, 1380–1471), "We need the same spirit to *understand* the Scripture which enabled the holy [ones] of old to *write* it."

Two—Reading in Community

- Ask: What are the benefits of reading the Bible in community with others?

Three—Salvation

This was John Wesley's purpose for reading Scripture.

- Ask: Why is salvation central to Christian life and faith?

Note that:

- John Wesley emphasized that the Bible is the primary book for the Christian and the church;
- Wesley also recommended additional resources that help Christians understand and clarify our beliefs; and
- the author provides information about these resources in the sections "What We Believe," "Doctrinal Materials," and "Contemporary Materials."

Creeds

Point out that:

- Creeds are statements of "What We Believe";
- The United Methodist Church shares the beliefs stated in Christian creeds, for example the Nicene Creed and the Apostles' Creed, with Christians around the globe; and
- the creeds date back to the early church and were written to combat heresies and clarify Christian beliefs.

Distribute *The United Methodist Hymnals* and instruct participants to turn to the Nicene Creed (#880) and the Apostles' Creed (#881) in the back of the hymnal.

Explain that the Nicene Creed was adopted by the Council of Nicaea in 325, then amended at the Council of Constantinople in 381. It affirms one God and the unity of God the Father, Son, and Holy Spirit.

The Apostles' Creed developed over time from questions of faith bishops asked persons who were being baptized. It likely appeared in its present form around the fifth century.

Invite the group to read the Nicene Creed and the Apostles' Creed together. Ask:

- What beliefs are stated in each creed?
- Why do you think it is important that these particular beliefs are affirmed?

Doctrinal Materials

Share these key points:

- Doctrinal materials explain or outline the doctrines or beliefs held by a particular group.
- "The Articles of Religion of the Methodist Church" is one doctrinal document that explains beliefs held by United Methodist Christians.
- This is one of the documents John Wesley gave Thomas Coke to take with him to America to support the ministry and work of Francis Asbury.

Distribute copies of the Articles of Religion or project the Articles from the website https://www.umc.org/en/content/articles-of-religion onto a screen.

Point out that these Articles explain the specific beliefs of Methodism and differ on various points from other denominations.

Read some or all of the Articles of Religion.

After each reading offer time for questions, observations, and comments. If questions are raised that cannot be answered by anyone in the group, ask for volunteers to research the questions and share their findings during the next session.

Contemporary Materials

Read the first sentence in the section titled "Contemporary Materials."

Distribute copies of "Our Social Creed" or project the creed onto a screen from https://www.umc.org/en/content/our-social-creed.

Read "Our Social Creed" together. You may also want to read "A Companion Litany to Our Social Creed" that follows the creed.

Offer time for questions, observations, and comments from the group.

Optional Activity—Our Theological Task: Interpreting Scripture to Participate in Service

In this section of chapter 5 the author discusses the four components of our theological task: Scripture, Tradition, Reason, and Experience.

Summarize Warner's key points.

Note that Scripture is the primary component.

Invite discussion of the following questions:

- How does Tradition facilitate your interpretation and study of Scripture?
- How does Reason facilitate your interpretation and study of Scripture?
- How does Experience facilitate your interpretation and study of Scripture?

Wrapping Up

Closing Activity

Invite the group to turn to the section "Catholic Spirit: Believing Deeply and Loving Well." Read the quote from Wesley's sermon printed there.

Invite discussion of this quote.

Closing Prayer

Holy and loving God, thank you for the Bible and for the creeds and other documents that help us grow in our faith. Be present with us and inspire us as we read and interpret Scripture. Let Scripture be our guide as we reach out in love and service to others. In the name of your Son, Jesus Christ, we pray. Amen.

SESSION 6

GROWING IN GRACE

Planning the Session

Session Goals

Through conversation, activities, and reflection, participants will:

- reflect on Methodism's distinctive characteristics:
  - ◊ grace extended to all,
  - ◊ community in small groups,
  - ◊ connection,
  - ◊ mission,
- consider how these distinctive characteristics equip us to meet the challenges facing The United Methodist Church today; and
- commit to living with hope as bearers of God's love and grace in the world.

Biblical Foundation

- Matthew 22:34-40

Before the Session

- Set up a table in the room with name tags, markers, Bibles, extra copies of *Knowing Who We Are*, paper and pencils, and the sign-in sheet.
- Write the heading "Challenges" on a board or chart paper. This will be used for the Leading into the Study activity.
- Have a whiteboard and markers, a chalkboard and chalk, or chart paper and markers available for use during the session.
- Read the Optional Activity and make preparations if you want to include it in your session plan. The Optional Activity for this session offers a time of review and consideration of next steps.

Getting Started

Opening Activities

Greet participants as they arrive. Invite them to make a name tag and pick up a Bible and/or copy of *Knowing Who We Are* if they do not have these.

Welcome participants and offer a time for introductions if there are newcomers.

Share any necessary information from the housekeeping list in Session 1. Remind the group to covenant together to respect a policy of confidentiality.

Leading into the Study

Remind the group of the purpose of this study by reading this paragraph from the introduction of *Knowing Who We Are*:

The purpose of this book is to offer those involved in church life a deeper understanding of the distinctives of Methodism to strengthen our sense of identity, better express our beliefs, and deepen our connections within The United Methodist Church. This study engages a set of important values and characteristics that make Wesleyan/Methodist Christianity distinctive— such as God's grace for all and sanctification as tangible transformation in individuals, communities, and creation.

If, during the last session, participants volunteered to do research related to questions about "The Articles of Religion of the Methodist Church" offer time for them to share their findings with the group.

Point out that the author begins chapter 6 by citing challenges that are facing our church, communities, country, and the world today.

Instruct the group to identify the challenges facing your local church and community. List these on the board or chart paper under the heading "Challenges."

You will refer to this list at the end of the session.

Opening Prayer

Holy and loving God, thank you for your gift of grace. Help us to extend your love and grace to others as we meet the challenges we face today. Help us to be mindful of the Holy Spirit working with us and through us as we follow the example of Jesus. In the name of your Son, Jesus Christ, we pray, Amen.

Learning Together

Video Study and Discussion

Play the video for Session 6. Discuss:

- Did anything specific stand out as you watched the video?
- What is something you learned or experienced that seems new or *renewed*?

Invite the group to keep both the video and the book in mind throughout the discussion below.

Bible Study and Discussion: Matthew 22:34-40

Growing in Grace: Responding to Challenges

Read, or invite a volunteer to read, Matthew 22:34-40.
Invite discussion of the following questions:

- When do you find it challenging to obey these two commandments?

- How does obeying the commandment to love our neighbor help us live out the Methodist characteristic of extending grace to all?

Read this quote from the introduction to chapter 6:

Growing in grace occurs when individuals and communities are open to the Triune God and participate in God's unfolding love and grace in the world.

Ask:

- How do love and grace contribute to the transformation of both individuals and communities? (It is important to note that the Holy Spirit works through us to bring about transformation.)

Book Study and Discussion

Highlight the three present-day challenges identified by the author:

- conflict,
- isolation and loneliness, and
- social needs.

Highlight these distinctive characteristics of Methodism that give United Methodists the capacity to respond to these current challenges:

- grace extended to all,
- community in small groups,
- connection, and
- mission.

Note that in the section "From Conflict to Community" the author identifies two aspects of our current situation: (1) deep conflicts in communities, and (2) "a default to the individual." She points out that Wesley's small groups chose to embrace Christian community in spite of disagreements.

Invite participants to refer to the section "From Conflict to Community" as they respond to these questions:

- What conflicts are creating division and turmoil in our churches and communities?
- How do we tend to "default to the individual"?

- How do the small groups to which you belong embrace Christian community?
- How might the model of Wesley's small groups help alleviate conflicts within your church and community?

Invite participants to turn to the section "From Isolation to Connection" as they respond to these questions:

- What statistics about loneliness in the United States surprised you or concerned you the most?
- What can our local church do today to minister to persons who feel isolated and experience loneliness?
- Why do we need the support and accountability of others to help us grow in love and grace?
- How can we reach out to persons who feel isolated and alone to welcome them into the fellowship of small groups within our church?

Remind the group that from the time of John and Charles Wesley, Methodists were interested in (1) the inner spiritual life and growing in faith, and (2) putting faith into practice by extending love and grace to others.

Invite the group to turn to the section "From Poverty to Sufficiency and Flourishing." Ask a volunteer to read the first paragraph with the statistics about poverty in the United States.

You may want to refer to chapter 4 and review (1) the work of the early Methodists as they addressed various social needs including education, health care, and alleviating poverty; and (2) recall the United Methodist institutions and organizations (for example, UMCOR, hospitals, schools) that address these issues today.

Invite your group to consider the areas of poverty and need in your own community. Ask:

- How are we as The United Methodist Church currently responding to the social needs in our community?

- What else might we do to address the needs of children, adults, and families who are living in poverty?

Call attention to the section titled "Grace *in* the Ashes: Looking Ahead in Hope" where the author writes about her experience of a fire on her family's property.

Read the invitation in the first paragraph of this section: "I invite us to look ahead with hope not despite our circumstances, but in the midst of them."

Call attention to the subtitles in this section that offer words of wisdom and guidance for times of crisis:

- In Times of Crisis: Collaborate
- Wet Blankets Can Actually Be Useful
- The Least Healthy Substance Burns Longest
- Uncontrollable Circumstances Are Inevitable
- God's Grace Always Persists

Refer to the list of challenges facing your church and community that the group compiled during the Leading into the Study activity. Consider each challenge separately and ask:

- How does the truth and wisdom expressed in these five subtitles offer us hope and guidance for ways to address this challenge?

Optional Activity— Knowing Who We Are: The Wesleyan Way of Grace

Read the title of the book, *Knowing Who We Are: The Wesleyan Way of Grace*.

Invite the group to think back over the topics covered in the book and the discussions and activities that were included in the sessions.

Invite discussion of these questions:

- How has this study strengthened your understanding of United Methodism?

- What did you learn about the history of Methodism that you did not know before?
- What did you learn about the current ministry and work of The United Methodist Church that you did not know before?
- How have you experienced God's prevenient, justifying, and sanctifying grace?
- How has your experience of God's grace transformed your life?
- How is God calling you to participate in God's ongoing work of transformation by sharing God's love and grace with others.

Wrapping Up

Closing Activity

Pray the Covenant Prayer printed at the end of chapter 6 together.

Closing Prayer

You may let the Covenant Prayer be the closing prayer or offer your own prayer for the final session of this study.

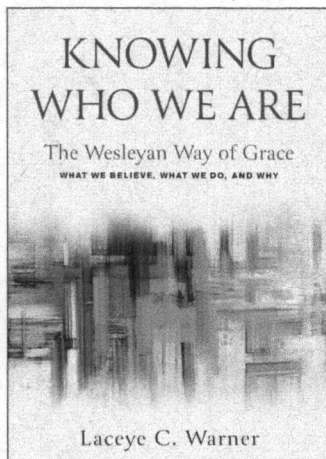